SPOOKY & DELICIOUS TREATS

BY HANNAH ABEDIKICHI

Copyright © 2020. All rights reserved. No part of this book may be reproduced in any form without written permission from the author. Reviewers may quote brief excerpts from the book in reviews.

Disclaimer: No part of this publication may be reproduced or transmitted in any form, mechanical or electronic, including photocopied or recorded, or by any information storage and retrieval system, or transmitted by email without permission in writing or email from the author or publisher.

While attempts have been made to verify all information provided in this publication, neither the author nor the publisher assumes any responsibility for errors, omissions, or contrary interpretations of the subjects discussed.

This book is for entertainment purposes only. The views expressed are those of the author alone and should not be taken as expert instructions or commands. The reader is responsible for his/her own actions.

Adherence to all applicable laws and regulations, including international, federal, state, and local government, or any other jurisdiction is the sole responsibility of the purchaser or reader.

Neither the author nor the publisher assume any responsibility or liability whatsoever on the behalf of the purchaser or reader of these materials.

TABLE OF CONTENTS

02   Skeleton Pops

05   Pumpkin Cinnamon Rolls

07   Hocus Pocus Spell Book Brownies

08   Dark Chocolate Halloween Cookies

10   Spider Peanut Butter Cookies

WWW.ABEDIKITCHEN.COM

Haunted Haysticks	12
Halloween Bark	13
Monster Cookie Dough Dip	14
Ghost Powdered Sugar Donuts	17
Worm Jello Cups	18
Ghost Bananas	19
Mandarin Spider	20
Pretzel Spider Webs	21
Pumpkin Rice Krispie Treats	22

24	Halloween Pretzel Rods
25	Monster Pudding Cups
26	Ghost Smores
27	Graveyard Dirt Cake
28	Witch Brooms
29	Bloody Finger Hotdogs
30	Halloween Pasta Salad
32	Spider Stuffed Mushrooms
34	Mummy Stuffed Jalapenos

Deviled Eggs	36
Mummy Dogs	38
Monster Spaghetti	40
Snake Breadsticks	42
Stuffed Halloween Peppers	44
Mouse Meatballs	46
Halloween Charcuterie Board	48
Spider Taco Dip	50

WWW.ABEDIKITCHEN.COM

INTRODUCTION

BY HANNAH ABEDIKICHI

Hello! My is Hannah Abedikichi, creator of Abedikitchen. I adore food. The only thing I love more than food is people. I am a mother to two beautiful kids and a wife to an amazing man, so I've got plenty of mouths to feed at home. In fact, cooking for my family is one of my greatest sources of joy.

I enjoy meals that are simple, healthy, and delicious. I've found that creating wholesome recipes helps me grow into the woman I always wanted to be.

Ultimately, my goal is to share simple, delicious recipes for REAL PEOPLE. I love food and I love sharing food things with people. Whether it is making food to share with my family and friends or sharing recipes and tips with people -- sharing food brings me so much joy.

Abedikitchen is a place where I share real life things. My recipes are not always perfect and they will sometimes be messy. But my hope is that my recipes will be a breath of fresh air and my books and blog are a place to find simple & delicious recipes for real people.

My mission is to simplify and uplift, one recipe at a time. I want to share recipes and other content that is simple and real life. I want to show the good side of things but also show the messy side.

Food is such a big part of EVERYONE's lives and it's one of the most favorite parts of my life. I like things to be simple. I want to help people feed their families delicious BUT super simple recipes. I like healthy recipes and eating healthy, but I love sharing the not-so-healthy things on occasion.

I want to be a place where people can come for food and recipe ideas that are familiar and simple, but delicious and fun.

"I LOVE FOOD AND COOKING SO MUCH AND I WANT TO SHARE THAT WITH PEOPLE."

INGREDIENTS

- Large marshmallows
- Black cookie icing
- Popsicle sticks
- White chocolate covered pretzels
- Mini marshmallows

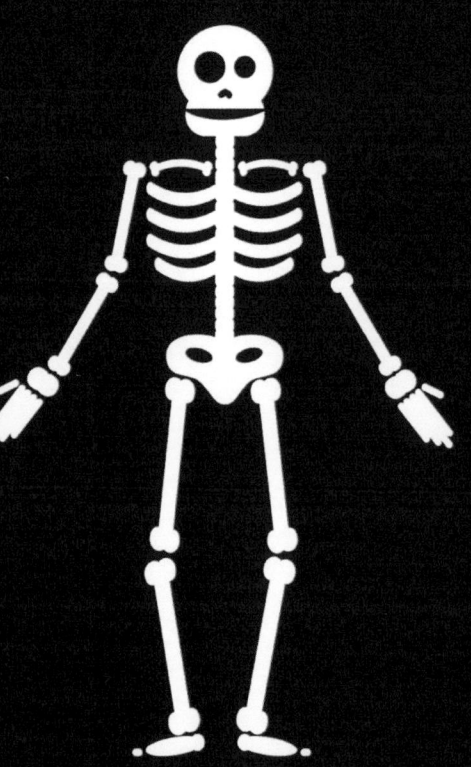

DIRECTIONS

- Using the cookie icing, make a skeleton face on each large marshmallow and let the icing dry.
- Place each skeleton face on the top of a popsicle stick.
- Thread 4 white chocolate covered pretzels onto each popsicle stick under the skeleton head.
- Push a mini marshmallow under the pretzels to secure them.

PUMPKIN CINNAMON ROLLS

INGREDIENTS

- 1 roll of Pillsbury cinnamon rolls
- 2 oz cream cheese, softened
- Green and orange food coloring

DIRECTIONS

- Place the cinnamon rolls on a greased baking sheet two inches apart. Pinch the top of each cinnamon roll to make it look like a stem.
- Bake according to package directions.
- While the cinnamon rolls are baking, put 1/4 of the icing that came with the rolls in a small bowl and the rest of it in another bowl. Add a little bit of cream cheese to each bowl and stir together well. Add green food coloring to the bowl with the least icing. Add orange food coloring to the bowl with the most icing. Stir together until evenly colored.
- Once the cinnamon rolls are finished cooking, remove them from the oven and let them cool for 2 minutes then ice the round part with orange icing and ice the stem part with green icing.
- Serve and enjoy!

HOCUS POCUS SPELL BOOK BROWNIES

INGREDIENTS

- 1/2 cup butter
- 3/4 cup sugar
- 2 eggs
- 3 tsp vanilla
- 3/4 cup cocoa powder
- 1/2 cup flour
- 1 tbsp instant espresso powder
- Black cookie icing
- Large candy eyes
- Piping bag

DIRECTIONS

- Preheat your oven to 350 degrees F.
- Line an 8x8 baking dish with parchment paper.
- Cream together the butter, sugar, vanilla, and eggs.
- Mix in the cocoa powder, flour, and espresso powder.
- Spread into a baking dish and bake for 20-25 minutes.
- Remove and let cool completely.
- Cut into bars.
- Decorate by placing the black cookie icing into a piping bag with a #2 tip or a small round tip.
- Pipe a small amount of icing onto the back of a large candy eye and place it in the middle of the brownie on the right side. Pipe icing onto the rest of the brownie to look like the Hocus Pocus Spell Book.

Dark Chocolate Halloween Cookies

INGREDIENTS

- 2 sticks of butter, at room temperature
- 3/4 cups packed brown sugar
- 1 cup sugar
- 2 eggs
- 1 tsp vanilla extract
- 2 cups all-purpose flour
- 3/4 cup cocoa powder
- 1 tsp baking soda
- 1 tsp baking powder
- 1/2 tsp salt
- 1 tsp instant espresso powder
- 1 cup dark chocolate chips
- 1 1/4 cups orange and yellow M&Ms

DIRECTIONS

- Preheat the oven to 350 degrees F.
- Cream together butter and sugar. Mix in the eggs and vanilla.
- In a separate bowl, mix together flour, cocoa, baking soda, baking powder, salt, and espresso powder.
- Add the dry ingredients to the wet ingredients.
- Stir in the chocolate chips and half of the M&Ms.
- Scoop onto greased or lined baking sheets with a 2 tbsp ice cream scooper.

DIRECTIONS

- Preheat the oven to 350 degrees F.
- Gently press the rest of the M&Ms onto the tops of the cookies.
- Bake for 8-10 minutes.

Spider Peanut Butter Cookies

INGREDIENTS

- 1/4 cup butter
- 1/2 cup creamy peanut butter
- 1/4 cup brown sugar
- 1/4 cup sugar
- 1 egg
- 1 tbsp milk
- 1 tsp vanilla
- 1 cup flour
- 1 tsp baking soda
- 1/2 tsp salt
- 1/4 cup sugar for rolling
- 24 mini Reese's cups, frozen
- 48 small candy eyes
- 1/2 cup chocolate chips
- Piping bag

DIRECTIONS

- Preheat your oven to 375 degrees Fahrenheit.
- In a large bowl, beat together the butter peanut butter egg, sugar, brown sugar, vanilla, and milk.
- In another bowl, whisk together the flour, baking soda, and salt.
- Slowly add the dry ingredients to the wet ingredients and mix until blended.
- Form into one-inch balls and place two inches apart on a cookie sheet.
- Bake for 10-12 minutes or until golden.
- Immediately after removing the cookies from the oven, press an upside-down frozen peanut butter cup in the center of each cookie then move to a cooling rack.
- Once you have moved the cookies to the cooling rack, place the candy eyes on the front of each Reese's cup.
- Refrigerate for 10 minutes to allow the cookies to become firm.
- Add chocolate chips to a piping bag and melt in the microwave.
- Clip a tiny piece of the corner of the bag off and draw eight legs for each spider.
- Refrigerate for 10 minutes then serve or store!

Haunted Haysticks

INGREDIENTS

- 1/3 cup purple candy melts
- 1/3 cup white candy melts
- 1/3 cup green candy melts
- 1/2 cup mini marshmallows
- 2 cups chow mein noodles
- 3/4 cup mini marshmallows
- Candy eyeballs- small, medium, and large

DIRECTIONS

- Get three small to medium bowls and add each color of candy melts to each. Evenly divide marshmallows between the bowls. Microwave each bowl at 30 second increments and stir until melted and combined well.
- Evenly divide the chow mein noodles between each bowl and stir to coat.
- Drop by rounded tablespoonfuls onto wax paper. Arrange candy eyeballs on one side of each treat. Let cool, then serve or store in an
- airtight container.

Halloween Bark

- 1 lb vanilla candy melts
- Mini pretzels
- Halloween Oreos
- Candy corn
- Halloween sprinkles
- Additional candies

DIRECTIONS

- Line a large baking sheet with parchment paper.
- Chop any large pieces of pretzels, candy, and Oreos.
- Melt the candy melts according to package directions.
- Pour half of the melted chocolate onto the baking sheet and spread evenly.
- Quickly add an assortment of pretzels, candy, and Oreos in a layer on the melted chocolate then add the remaining melted chocolate on top.
- Add any remaining pretzels, candies, and Oreos; along with sprinkles.
- Place the baking sheet in the freezer and let sit for 10 minutes.
- Break into pieces and serve or store in an airtight container.

Monster Cookie Dough Dip

INGREDIENTS

- 8 oz cream cheese, at room temperature
- 1/2 cup salted butter, at room temperature
- 1 cup creamy peanut butter
- 1 cup light brown sugar, packed
- 1 1/2 cups powdered sugar
- 1/4 tsp salt
- 1 cup M&Ms
- 1 cup chocolate chips
- Graham crackers, animal crackers, or pretzels; for serving

DIRECTIONS

- In a large bowl, mix together cream cheese, butter, and peanut butter.
- Add in the brown sugar, powdered sugar, and salt. Beat on high until light and fluffy.
- Stir in M&Ms and chocolate chips.
- Pour into a serving bowl and serve with graham crackers, animal crackers, or pretzels.

Ghost Powdered Sugar Donuts

INGREDIENTS

- 1 package refrigerated biscuits
- 2 cups vegetable oil
- 2 cups powdered sugar
- Soda top or sjmilar item

DIRECTIONS

- Unroll the biscuits from the package and place them on a sheet of wax or parchment paper.
- Roll each biscuit into a long oval using a rolling pin or a glass cup.
- Use a soda top and cut out ghost eyes and mouth.
- Pour oil into a large skillet over medium heat.
- When oil is hot, place each ghost in the skillet. Work in batches to not overcrowd the skillet. Cook until each side is golden brown.
- Remove the ghosts to a plate with paper towels.
- Place the powdered sugar in a large ziplock bag.
- Place the ghosts in the ziplock bag and shake until the ghosts are covered.
- Remove from sugar and serve.

INGREDIENTS

- 3 oz package of green jello (any flavor will work)
- Gummy worms

Worm Jello Cups

DIRECTIONS

- Prepare the jello according to package directions.
- Before letting the jello refrigerate to set, place 2-3 gummy worms in clear plastic or clear glass cups. Place 1 or 2 in the bottom and let one hang over the side. Pour the liquid jello mixture into the cups. Place the cups in the refrigerator to set then serve.

INGREDIENTS

- 4 bananas
- 1/4 cup chocolate chips

Ghost Bananas

DIRECTIONS

- Peel the bananas and cut each one in half.
- Melt the chocolate chips and spoon them into a piping bag. Cut the end of the bag and pipe ghost eyeballs and mouths onto the bananas.

Mandarine Spider

INGREDIENTS

- 3 oranges
- Googly eyes

Create a spider with the oranges as seen above.

PRETZEL SPIDER WEBS

INGREDIENTS

- White chocolate chips
- Pretzel sticks
- Piping bag
- Parchment paper

DIRECTIONS

- Place parchment paper on the counter.
- Take 8 pretzel sticks and group them together to form a circle.
- Repeat with desired amount of spider webs.
- Melt white chocolate chips in a bowl in the microwave then transfer to a piping bag.
- Pipe a spiral over the pretzel circles to resemble a spider web.

Pumpkin Rice Krispie Treats

INGREDIENTS

- 6 cups rice krispies cereal
- 3 tbsp salted butter
- 10 oz package of mini marshmallows
- Orange gel food coloring
- 3 pretzel rods, broken into 2-inch pieces
- White melting chocolate
- Green gel food coloring

DIRECTIONS

- Pour rice krispies cereal into a large bowl.
- Melt butter in a 4-quart nonstick saucepan over medium low heat.
- Add marshmallows to the saucepan and stir until melted. Add orange gel food coloring until desired color is reached. Stir together well.
- Remove from heat and immediately pour rice krispies into marshmallow mixture and gently stir until cereal is evenly coated. Let cool slightly.
- Spray your hands with non-stick cooking spray and shape into balls about the size of a baseball. Insert 1 piece of pretzel rod into the top center and shape to look more pumpkin-like. Transfer to a plate.
- In a small bowl, melt white melting chocolate. Add green food coloring and stir until mixed evenly. Place the green melting chocolate in a piping bag and cut a small piece from the end. Pipe a leaf next to the pretzel stem.

Halloween Pretzel Rods

INGREDIENTS

- Pretzel rods
- Various colors of melting chocolate
- Various food decorations such candy corn, sprinkles, etc.

DIRECTIONS

- Melt each color of melting chocolate.
- Dip pretzel rods in desired colors and place on wax paper.
- Before the chocolate dries, decorate.

MONSTER PUDDING CUPS

- 3.4 oz package of butterscotch pudding
- 2 brownies
- 4 large marshmallows
- 1/4 cup chocolate chips

- Prepare the butterscotch pudding according to package directions.
- Chop the brownie into small pieces.
- When the pudding is ready, fill 4 small clear plastic cups about 1/4 of the way full with pudding. Add a layer of chopped brownie to each cup. Then, add another layer of pudding.
- Cut each marshmallow in half and top the cups with them.
- Melt the chocolate chips and spoon them into a piping bag. Cut the end of the bag and pipe eyeballs onto the marshmallows.

Ghost Smores

INGREDIENTS

- Graham crackers
- Marshmallows
- Hershey's chocolate bars or any chocolate square style candy bar that you prefer

DIRECTIONS

- Preheat your oven to 350 degrees F.
- Half the graham crackers and lay them out.
- Place chocolate squares on the graham cracker halves.
- Top each chocolate square with a ghost marshmallow.
- Top each marshmallow with another graham cracker square.
- Bake in the oven for 5-10 minutes.

Graveyard Dirt Cake

INGREDIENTS

- 3 5 oz cans of evaporated milk
- 5 oz box of chocolate pudding
- 1 package oreos, crushed
- 1/4 cup melted butter
- Ghost and pumpkin candies
- Small clear glass or clear plastic cups

DIRECTIONS

- In a large bowl, mix the evaporated milk and chocolate pudding mix. Mix with an electric mixer for 2 minutes.
- In a medium bowl, mix crushed Oreos and melted butter. Top each cup with Oreo butter mixture.
- Place a small layer of crushed Oreo mixture into the bottom of each cup. Spoon the pudding mixture into cups. Spoon another layer of Oreo mixture over the pudding.
- Place a ghost and pumpkin in each cup then serve.

Witch Brooms

INGREDIENTS

- Pretzel sticks
- Cheese sticks, cut in 1 inch pieces
- Green onions

DIRECTIONS

- Cut green onions into long skinny strips
- Slightly fan out the ends of each cheese stick piece to resemble bristles of a broom.
- Stick a pretzel stick into each cheese stick piece.
- Tie a green onion onto the cheese and trim the excess.

BLOODY FINGER HOTDOGS

INGREDIENTS

- 6 hot dogs
- 6 hot dog buns
- Ketchup

DIRECTIONS

- Add water to a medium sized pot and bring to a boil.
- Slice the hot dogs to look like fingers.
- Boil the hotdogs for 5 minutes.
- Place each "finger" into a hotdog bun loaded with ketchup and add more ketchup to the bottom of each "finger".

Halloween Pasta Salad

- 1 lb rotini pasta
- Black gel food coloring
- 1 cucumber sliced
- 1/2 head of broccoli, chopped small
- 1 cup cherry tomatoes, halved
- 1 cup shredded carrots
- 1 cup shredded cheddar cheese
- Italian salad dressing, to taste

- Cook the pasta al dente according to package directions. Save 1/4 cup pasta water.
- Place the pasta and 1/4 cup pasta water in a large bowl. Add black gel food coloring and stir until pasta is black.
- Drain off any excess water.
- Use a knife to cut Jack-O-Lantern faces into the cucumber slices.
- Add the remaining ingredients to the pasta and stir.
- Top with sliced cucumbers before serving.

Easy Ways to Make Food More Fun

Be creative and have fun with your food. You can easily jazz up simple foods with googly eyes, cutting shapes and faces into the foods, or adding weird combinations together. There are no rules when it comes to creativity!

Spider Stuffed Mushrooms

INGREDIENTS

- 24 whole baby bella mushrooms, washed and stems removed
- 8 oz cream cheese, softened
- 1 cup shredded cheddar cheese
- 8 oz cooked ground sausage
- Garlic powder, salt, and pepper; to taste

DIRECTIONS

- Preheat your oven or grill to 375 degrees F.
- Place mushroom caps, stem side down on a rimmed baking sheet (or on a grill pan) and cook for 15 minutes. Remove from the oven or grill and set aside.
- Mix together the cream cheese, cheddar cheese, sausage, garlic, salt, and pepper.
- Turn mushrooms stem side up and divide the sausage mixture evenly between the mushrooms.
- Cut 12 olives in half lengthwise. Place 1 half of an olive in the center of each mushroom. Cut the remaining olives into spider legs. Arrange 8 spider legs around each olive half to resemble a spider.
- Cook or grill for an additional 8 minutes until the filling is hot.

MUMMY STUFFED JALAPENOS

INGREDIENTS

- 6 large jalapeno peppers
- 2 oz feta cheese
- 4 oz cream cheese, at room temperature
- 4 oz shredded cheddar cheese
- 2 tbsp chopped fresh parsley
- Garlic powder, salt, and pepper; to taste
- 6 strips of bacon
- 24 candy eyes

DIRECTIONS

- Preheat your oven or grill to 425 degrees F.
- Cut the peppers in half lengthwise and scoop out the seeds.
- Stir together the feta, cream cheese, shredded cheddar cheese, parsley, onion powder, salt, and pepper.
- Stuff the peppers with the mixture.
- Slice the bacon in half lengthwise.

MUMMY STUFFED JALAPENOS
continued...

DIRECTIONS

- Wrap the bacon around the peppers, leaving a small space at the top of each pepper to add the eyes at the end of cooking.
- Place on a baking sheet and cook for 15 – 20 minutes or until the bacon is cooked.
- Remove from the oven and let the peppers cool for a few minutes.
- Add the candy eyes.

Deviled Eggs

INGREDIENTS

- 6 large eggs
- Black food coloring gel
- 2 beets
- Olive oil
- Salt and pepper

 DIRECTIONS

- Place the eggs in a pot of water and bring to a boil. Remove from heat and let sit for 7 minutes.
- Place some cool water in a large bowl. After the eggs have sat in the hot water for 7 minutes, add them to the cool water until they are cool enough to handle.
- Gently tap each egg on your counter then gently roll them to crack the shells, but don't remove them yet.
- Add black food coloring gel to the bowl of cool water and stir. After you get all the eggs cracked, place them in the bowl with black water.
- Refrigerate the bowl for 7 hours or overnight.
- When you are almost ready to remove the eggs from the refrigerator, peel and dice the beets. Toss with olive oil and season with salt and pepper. Bake at 400 degrees F for 25 minutes or until easily pierced with a fork. Remove them from the oven and let them cool slightly.
- Transfer the beets to a food processor.
- Remove the shells from the eggs and cut each egg in half lengthwise.
- Remove the yolks from the eggs and add them to the food processor with the beets.
- Pulse together the beets and egg yolks until smooth.
- Place the filling on the egg halves and refrigerate for at least 2 hours before serving.

DIRECTIONS

- Preheat your oven to 375 degrees F.
- Open the crescent roll package and roll out the dough. Press on the perforations to seal the dough together into one large rectangle.
- Cut the dough into 1/4 inch strips using a pizza cutter.
- Wrap the pieces of dough around each hotdog to look like mummy bandages. Leave gaps at the top for the eyes.
- Place each wrapped hotdog on a baking sheet and bake for 10-12 minutes or until the dough is golden brown.
- Remove from the oven and let cool for a couple minutes. Add a small dot of ketchup or mustard on the back of each candy eye and place on the mummy dogs.

INGREDIENTS

- 6 hot dogs
- 1 package crescent roll dough
- 12 candy eyes

Monster Spaghetti

- 1 lb ground Italian sausage
- 1 onion, diced
- 15 oz can of crushed tomatoes
- 15 oz can of diced tomatoes
- 28 oz can of pasta sauce
- 1/2 tsp salt
- 1/4 tsp pepper
- 1/2 tsp garlic powder
- 1/2 tsp Italian seasoning
- 1 lb spaghetti pasta
- Black gel food coloring
- Green olives

- In a large saucepan, brown the Italian sausage and drain off any fat. Cook the diced onion with the Italian sausage.
- Add the crushed tomatoes, diced tomatoes, pasta sauce, and seasonings to the saucepan and bring to a boil.
- Reduce heat and let simmer for 20 minutes.
- While the sauce is simmering, bring a large pot of water to a boil. Add salt. Add pasta and cook to al dente according to package directions. Save 1/2 cup pasta water.
- Drain the pasta then add it to a large bowl. Add several dots of food coloring and about 1/4 cup of pasta water. Stir until pasta is evenly colored black.
- Serve sauce over black pasta.
- Add olives as monster eyes. (optional)

Snake Breadsticks

- 1 package refrigerated pie crust
- Sesame seed mix
- Nonstick spray
- Wooden chopsticks
- Cherry tomatoes or red bell pepper
- Black olives

Pressy's Tips

This side pairs well with the monster spaghetti on page 40.

- Preheat your oven to 350 degrees F.
- Open the pie crust and lay out on a flat surface.
- Slice into 12 long strips.
- Spray each chopstick with nonstick spray then wrap each pie crust strip around each chopstick.

CONTINUED...

- Flatten out one end of each breadstick to resemble a snake's head and taper the other end to resemble a tail.
- Sprinkle with sesame seed mix.
- Cut cherry tomatoes or red bell peppers to resemble snake tongues and cut black olives to resemble snake eyes and place on the snake heads.

Pressy's Tips

You can also use this recipe to make Harry Potter magic wands!

Stuffed Halloween Peppers

- Green, orange, and yellow bell peppers
- 1 cup sliced mushrooms
- Sirloin steak
- 1/2 red onion
- 1 red bell pepper, sliced
- Provolone cheese slices
- Olive oil
- Salt and Pepper

- Preheat your oven to 400 degrees F and line a 9x13 inch baking dish with foil.
- Cut the bell peppers as you see in the pictures. Cut the "face" off the peppers then cut the Frankenstein face on the green pepper, the Jack-O-Lantern onto the orange pepper, and the ghost onto the yellow bell pepper. Drizzle them with olive oil and season with salt and pepper. Bake for 10 minutes in the lined baking dish.

- Heat a pan with olive oil and cook the steak and then slice very thinly.
- In the same pan, sauté the mushrooms, onions, and sliced red bell pepper. Add in the sliced steak and set aside.
- Remove the green, orange, and yellow bell peppers from the oven and divide the sliced steak and veggies evenly between the peppers.
- Top with cheese and bake for 15 minutes then top with the "faces" and serve.

Pressy's Tips

You can fill the peppers with anything you like. Have fun and be creative!

Mouse Meatballs

- 1 lb ground italian sausage
- 1 large egg, beaten
- 1/4 cup breadcrumbs
- 1/4 cup grated parmesan cheese
- 2 tsp minced garlic
- 1/2 tsp salt
- Whole peppercorns
- 1 carrot, thinly sliced
- Toothpicks

- Preheat your oven to 400 degrees F. Line a baking sheet with foil and spray with nonstick spray.
- In a large bowl, combine the ground sausage, egg, breadcrumbs, cheese, salt, garlic, and salt. Stir to combine but do not overmix.
- Scoop out long oval shaped meatballs (shaped as they are in the picture).
- Bake for 20-22 minutes, turning halfway through cook time.
- When you've removed them from the oven, place peppercorns for the nose and eyes and carrot slices for the ears. Place toothpicks for the tails.

Halloween Charcuterie Board

Halloween charcuterie boards are perfect for this spooky season. You can really be creative with these boards and go as big or small as you want to. All you need is a wooden board to put the food on.

Here are some ideas for things to add to your charcuterie board:

- meats
- cheeses
- nuts
- fruits
- crackers
- jams or jellies
- olives
- peppers
- halloween candy
- herbs
- halloween decorations like plastic spiders, skeletons, etc.

Spider Taco Dip

- 1 lb ground beef
- 15 oz can of refried beans
- 2 packages taco seasoning, divided
- 8 oz cream cheese, softened
- 16 oz sour cream, divided
- 4 oz can of green chiles
- 15 oz jar of chunky salsa
- 1 1/4 cup shredded cheese, divided
- 1 cup guacamole
- 1 tomato, diced
- 2 green onions, sliced
- 2 tbsp black olives, diced
- Tortilla chips

- **Layer 1:** Mix 8 oz cream cheese, 1 cup of sour cream, and 1 package of taco seasoning until smooth. Spread into the bottom of a round pie dish.
- **Layer 2:** Brown ground beef in a skillet over medium high heat. Drain off the grease and add 1 package of taco seasoning and 1 to 2 tbsp of water if needed but make sure you do not make it very liquid. Spread the meat over the first layer.
- **Layer 3:** Heat the refried beans to make them easier to spread and carefully spread them over the meat layer.
- **Layer 4:** Spread the diced green chiles over the refried bean layer.
- **Layer 5**: Spread the salsa over the green chiles. Make sure to use a thick and chunky layer to reduce liquid.
- **Layer 6:** Sprinkle 1 cup of cheese over the salsa layer.
- **Layer 7:** Spread guacamole over the cheese layer.
- **Top Layer:** Spoon 1 cup of sour cream into a Ziplock bag and cut off a small piece of one corner and pipe the sour cream onto the guacamole layer, making it look like a spider web. Then, sprinkle diced tomatoes, green onions, black olives, and remaining cheddar cheese to the edges of the dip.
- Serve with tortilla chips.

Printed in Dunstable, United Kingdom